15/01/21

Zadie Smith is the author of five novels, three collections of essays and a collection of short stories. She has won literary awards including the James Tait Black Memorial Prize, the Orange Prize for Fiction, the Whitbread First Novel Award and the *Guardian* First Book Award, and has been shortlisted for the Man Booker Prize and the Baileys Women's Prize for Fiction. Zadie Smith is a Member of the American Academy of Arts and Letters and the Royal Society of Literature. She is a regular contributor to the *New Yorker* and the *New York Review of Books*.

By the same author

FICTION
White Teeth
The Autograph Man
On Beauty
NW
The Embassy of Cambodia
Swing Time
Grand Union (*stories*)

NON-FICTION
The Book of Other People (*editor*)
Changing My Mind: Occasional Essays
Feel Free

INTIMATIONS

Six Essays

Zadie Smith

PENGUIN BOOKS

PENGUIN BOOKS

UK | USA | Canada | Ireland | Australia
India | New Zealand | South Africa

Penguin Books is part of the Penguin Random House group of companies
whose addresses can be found at global.penguinrandomhouse.com.

First published 2020
002

'The American Exception' was first published in the *New Yorker* in 2020.
Words from 'Lovefool', on p. 78, by Peter Svensson and Nina Persson.

Set in 11.5/14 pt Fournier MT Std
Typeset by Jouve (UK), Milton Keynes
Printed and bound in Great Britain by Clays Ltd, Elcograf S.p.A.

A CIP catalogue record for this book is available from the British Library

ISBN: 978-0-241-49238-3

www.greenpenguin.co.uk

Penguin Random House is committed to a
sustainable future for our business, our readers
and our planet. This book is made from Forest
Stewardship Council® certified paper.

For Jackie and Jay

It stares you in the face. No role is so well suited to philosophy as the one you happen to be in right now.

Marcus Aurelius

My vocabulary is adequate for writing notes and keeping journals but absolutely useless for an active moral life.

Grace Paley

Contents

Foreword   xi

1   Peonies   1

2   The American Exception   11

3   Something to Do   19

4   Suffering Like Mel Gibson   29

5   Screengrabs   37
(*After* Berger, before the virus)

   A Man with Strong Hands

   A Character in a Wheelchair
   in the Vestibule

   A Woman with a Little Dog

   A Hovering Young Man

   An Elder at the 98 Bus Stop

   A Provocation in the Park

   Postscript: Contempt as a Virus

6   Intimations   73

All the author's royalties will go to charity. This edition benefits:

The Equal Justice Initiative

The Covid-19 Emergency Relief Fund for New York

Foreword

There will be many books written about the year 2020: historical, analytical, political as well as comprehensive accounts. This is not any of those – the year isn't halfway done. What I've tried to do is organize some of the feelings and thoughts that events, so far, have provoked in me, in those scraps of time the year itself has allowed. These are above all personal essays: small by definition, short by necessity.

Early on in the crisis, I picked up Marcus Aurelius and for the first time in my life read his *Meditations* not as an academic exercise, nor in pursuit of pleasure, but with the same attitude I bring to the instructions for a flat-pack table – I was in need of practical assistance. (That the assistance Aurelius offers is for the spirit makes it no less practical in my view.) Since that moment, one form of crisis has collided with another, and I am no more a Stoic now than I was when I opened that ancient book. But I did come out with two invaluable intimations. Talking to yourself can be useful. And writing means being overheard.

31 May 2020
London

Peonies

Just before I left New York, I found myself in an unex-
pected position: clinging to the bars of the Jefferson
Market Garden, looking in. A moment before I'd been
on the run as usual, intending to exploit two minutes of
time I'd carved out of the forty-five-minute increments
into which, back then, I divided my days. Each block of
time packed tight and levelled off precisely, like a child
prepping a sandcastle. Two 'free' minutes meant a mac-
chiato. (In an ideal, cashless world, if nobody spoke to
me.) In those days, the sharp end of my spade was
primed against chatty baristas, overly friendly mothers,
needy students, curious readers – anyone I considered
a threat to the programme. Oh, I was very well defended.
But this was a sneak attack . . . by horticulture. Tulips.
Springing up in a little city garden, from a triangle of
soil where three roads met. Not a very sophisticated
flower – a child could draw it – and these were garish:
pink with orange highlights. Even as I was peering in
at them I wished they were peonies.

City born, city bred, I wasn't aware of having an

especially keen interest in flowers – at least no interest strong enough to forgo coffee. But my fingers were curled around those iron bars. I wasn't letting go. Nor was I alone. Either side of Jefferson stood two other women, both around my age, staring through the bars. The day was cold, bright, blue. Not a cloud between the World Trade and the old seven-digit painted phone number for Bigelow's. We all had somewhere to be. But some powerful instinct had drawn us here, and the predatory way we were ogling those tulips put me in mind of Nabokov, describing the supposed genesis of *Lolita*: 'As far as I can recall, the initial shiver of inspiration was somehow prompted by a newspaper story about an ape in the Jardin des Plantes, who, after months of coaxing by a scientist, produced the first drawing ever charcoaled by an animal: this sketch showed the bars of the poor creature's cage.' I've always been interested in that quote – without believing a word of it. (Something inspired *Lolita*. I'm certain no primates were involved.) The scientist offers the piece of charcoal expecting or hoping for a transcendent revelation about this ape, but the revelation turns out to be one of contingency, of a certain set of circumstances – of things as they happen to be. The ape is caged in by its nature, by its instincts, and by its circumstance. (Which of these takes the primary role is for zoologists to debate.) So it goes. I didn't need a Freudian to tell me that three middle-aged women, teetering at the brink of peri-menopause, had been drawn to a gaudy symbol of fertility and renewal in the middle of a barren concrete metropolis . . . and, indeed, when we three spotted each other there were shamefaced smiles all round. But in my case the shame was not what it would have once been, back in the day – back when I first read *Lolita*, as a young woman. At that time, the cage of my circumstance, in my mind, was my gender. Not its actuality – I liked my body well enough. What I didn't like was what I thought it signified: that I was tied to my 'nature', to my animal body – to the whole simian realm of instinct – and far more elementally so than, say, my brothers. I had 'cycles'. They did not. I was to pay attention to 'clocks'. They needn't. There were special words for me, lurking on the horizon, prepackaged to mark the possible future stages of my existence. I might become a spinster. I might become a crone. I might be a babe or a MILF or 'childless'. My brothers, no matter what else might befall them, would remain men. And in the end of it all, *if I was lucky*, I would become that most piteous of things, an old lady, whom I already understood was a figure everybody felt free to patronize, even children.

'(You Make Me Feel Like) A Natural Woman' – I used to listen to that song and try to imagine its counterpart. You could make someone feel like a 'real' man – no doubt its own kind of cage – but never a natural one. A man was a man was a man. He bent nature to his will. He did not submit to it, except in death.

Submission to nature was to be my realm, but I wanted no part of that, and so would refuse to keep any track whatsoever of my menstrual cycle, preferring to cry on Monday and find out the (supposed) reason for my tears on Tuesday. Yes, much better this than to properly prepare for a blue Monday or believe it in any way inevitable. My moods were my own. They had no reflection in nature. I refused to countenance the idea that anything about me might have a cyclic, monthly motion. And if I had children one day, I would have them 'on my own timeline', irrespective of how the bells were tolling on all those dreaded clocks in the women's magazines. Of 'broodiness' I would hear nothing: I was not a hen. And if, when I was in my twenties, any bold Freudian had dared to suggest that my apartment – filled as it was with furry cushions and furry rugs and furry bolsters, furry throws and furry footstools – in any sense implied a sublimated desire for animal company, or that I was subconsciously feathering my nest in expectation of new life, well, I would have shown that impertinent Freudian the door. I was a woman, but not *that* kind of woman. 'Internalized misogyny', I suppose they'd call all of the above now. I have no better term. But at the hot core of it there was an obsession with control, common amongst my people (writers).

Writing is routinely described as 'creative' – this has never struck me as the correct word. Planting tulips is creative. To plant a bulb (I imagine, I've never done it) is to participate in some small way in the cyclic miracle of creation. Writing is control. The part of the university in which I teach should properly be called the Controlling Experience Department. Experience – mystifying, overwhelming, conscious, subconscious – rolls over everybody. We try to adapt, to learn, to accommodate, sometimes resisting, other times submitting to, whatever confronts us. But writers go further: they take this largely shapeless bewilderment and pour it into a mould of their own devising. Writing is *all* resistance. Which can be a handsome, and sometimes even a useful, activity – on the page. But, in my experience, turns out to be a pretty hopeless practice for real life. In real life, submission and resistance have no predetermined shape. Even more befuddling, to a writer like me, is that the values normally associated with those words on a page – submission, negative; resistance, positive – cannot be relied upon out in the field. Sometimes it is right to submit to love, and wrong to resist affection. Sometimes it is wrong to resist disease and right to submit to the inevitable. And vice versa. Each novel you read (never mind the novels you write) will give you some theory of which attitude is best to strike at which moment, and – if you experience enough of them – will provide you, at the very least, with a wide repertoire of possible attitudes. But out in the field, experience has no chapter headings or paragraph breaks or ellipses in which to catch your breath . . . it just keeps coming at you.

Now, more than ever – to use a popular narrative mould – I know that. It happens that the day I was drawn to those tulips was a few days before the global humbling began – one that arrived equally for men and women both – but in my own shallow puddle of experience it's these dumb tulips that served as a tiny, early preview of what I now feel every moment of every day, that is, the complex and ambivalent nature of 'submission'. If only it were possible to simply state these feelings without insisting on them, without making an argument or a dogma out of them! *This* type of woman and *that* type of woman – just so many life rings thrown to a drowning Heraclitus. Each one a different form of fiction. Is it possible to be as flexible on the page – as shamelessly self-forgiving and ever-changing – as we are in life? We can't seem to find the way. Instead, to write is to swim in an ocean of hypocrisies, moment by moment. We know we are deluded, but the strange thing is that this delusion is necessary, if only temporarily, to create the mould in the first place, the one into which you pour everything you can't give shape to in life. This is all better said by Kierkegaard, in a parable:

'The Dog Kennel by the Palace'

To what shall we compare the relation between the thinker's system and his actual existence?
A thinker erects an immense building, a system, a system which embraces the whole of existence and world-history etc. – and if we contemplate his personal life, we discover to our astonishment this terrible and ludicrous fact, that he himself personally does not live in this immense high-vaulted palace, but in a barn alongside of it, or in a dog kennel, or at the most in the porter's lodge. If one were to take the liberty of calling his attention to this by a single word, he would be offended. For he has no fear of being under a delusion, if only he can get the system completed . . . . by means of the delusion.

They were tulips. I wanted them to be peonies. In my story, they are, they will be, they were and will for ever be peonies – for, when I am writing, space and time itself bend to my will! Through the medium of tenses! In real life, the dog kennel is where I make my home. When I was a kid, I thought I'd rather be a brain in a jar than a 'natural woman'. I have turned out to be some odd combination of both, from moment to moment, and with no control over when and where or why those moments occur. Whether the 'natural' part of my woman-hood is an essential biological fact or an expression (as de Beauvoir argued) of an acculturation so deep it looks very much like roots growing out of the bulb, at this point in my life I confess I don't know and I don't care. I am not a scientist or a sociologist. I'm a novelist. Who can admit, late in the day, during this strange and overwhelming season of death that collides, outside my window, with the emergence of dandelions, that spring sometimes rises in me, too, and the moon may occasionally tug at my moods, and if I hear a strange baby cry some part of me still leaps to attention – to submission. And once in a while a vulgar strain of spring flower will circumvent a long-trained and self-consciously strict downtown aesthetic. Just before an unprecedented April arrives and makes a nonsense of every line.

The American Exception

He speaks truth so rarely that when you hear it from his own mouth – 29 March 2020 – it has the force of revelation: 'I wish we could have our old life back. We had the greatest economy that we've ever had, and we didn't have death.'

Well, maybe not the whole, unvarnished truth. The first clause was neither true nor false: it described only a desire. A desire which, when I heard it – and found its bleating echo in myself – I'll admit I weighed in my hand, for a moment, like a shiny apple. It sounded like a decent 'wartime' wish, war being the analogy he's chosen to use. But no one in 1945 wished to return to the 'old life', to return to 1939 – except to resurrect the dead. Disaster demanded a new dawn. Only new thinking can lead to a new dawn. We know that. Yet as he said it – 'I wish we could have our old life back' – he caught his audience in a moment of weakness: in their dressing gowns, weeping, or on a work call, or with a baby on their hip *and* a work call, or putting on a home-made hazmat suit to brave the subway, on the way to work that cannot be done at home, while millions of bored children climbed the walls from coast to coast. And, yes, in that brittle context, the 'old life' had a comforting sound, if only rhetorically, like 'once upon a time' or 'but I LOVE him!' The second clause brought me back to my senses. Snake oil, snake oil, snake oil. The Devil is consistent, if nothing else. I dropped that apple, and, lo, it was putrid and full of worms.

Then he spoke the truth: *we didn't have death.*

We had dead people. We had casualties and we had victims. We had more or less innocent bystanders. We had body counts and sometimes even photos in the newspapers of body bags, though many felt it was wrong to show them. We had 'unequal health outcomes'. But, in America, all of these involved some culpability on the part of the dead. Wrong place, wrong time. Wrong skin colour. Wrong side of the tracks. Wrong ZIP code, wrong beliefs, wrong city. Wrong position of hands when asked to exit the vehicle. Wrong health insurance – or none. Wrong attitude to the police officer. What we were completely missing, however, was the concept of death itself, death absolute. The kind of death that comes to us all, irrespective of position. Death absolute is the truth of our existence as a whole, of course, but America has rarely been philosophically inclined to consider existence as a whole, preferring instead to attack death as a series of discrete problems. Wars on drugs, cancer, poverty, and so on. Not that there is anything ridiculous about trying to lengthen the distance between the dates on our birth certificates and the ones on our tombstones: ethical life depends on the meaningfulness of that effort. But perhaps nowhere in the world has this effort – and its relative success – been linked so emphatically to money as it is in America.

Maybe this is why plagues – being considered insufficiently hierarchical in nature, too inattentive to income disparity – were long ago relegated to history in the American imagination, or to other continents. In fact, as he made clear early on in his Presidency, entire 'shit-hole' countries were to be considered culpable for their own high death rates – they were by definition in the wrong place (over there) at the wrong time (an earlier stage of development). Such places were plagued in the permanent sense, by not having the foresight to be America. Even global mass extinction – in the form of environmental collapse – was not going to reach America, or would reach it only ultimately, at the very last minute. Relatively secure, in its high-walled haven, America would feast on whatever was left of its resources, still great by comparison with the suffering out there, beyond its borders.

But now, as he so rightly points out, we are great with death – we are mighty with it. There is a fear, when all of this is said and done, that America will lead the world in it. And yet, perversely, the supposed democratic nature of plague – the way in which it can strike all registered voters equally – turns out to be somewhat overstated. A plague it is, but American hierarchies, hundreds of years in the making, are not so easily over-turned. Amid the great swathe of indiscriminate death, some old American distinctions persist. Black and Latino people are now dying at twice the rate of white and Asian people. More poor people are dying than rich. More in urban centres than in the country. The virus map of the New York boroughs turns redder along pre-cisely the same lines as it would if the relative shade of crimson counted not infection and death but income brackets and middle-school ratings. Untimely death has rarely been random in these United States. It has usu-ally had a precise physiognomy, location and bottom line. For millions of Americans, it's always been a war.

Now, apparently for the first time, he sees it. And, in a hurry for glory, he calls himself a wartime President. Let him take that title, as the British Prime Minister, across the ocean, likewise attempts to place himself in the Churchillian role. Churchill (who actually fulfilled his wartime role) learned the hard way that even when the people follow you into war, and even when they agree you've had a 'good' war, this does not necessarily mean they want to return to the 'old life', or be led by you into the new one. War transforms its participants. What was once necessary appears inessential; what was taken for granted, unappreciated and abused now reveals itself to be central to our existence. Strange inversions proliferate. People find themselves applauding a national health service that their own government criminally underfunded and neglected these past ten years. People thank God for 'essential' workers they once considered lowly, who not so long ago they despised for wanting fifteen bucks an hour.

Death has come to America. It was always here, albeit obscured and denied, but now everybody can see it. The 'war' that America is waging against it has no choice but to go above, around and beyond an empty figurehead. This is a collective effort; there are millions of people involved in it, and they won't easily forget what they have seen. They won't forget the abject, exceptionally American, predicament of watching individual states, as New York Governor Andrew Cuomo memorably put it, bidding as if 'on eBay' for life-saving equipment. Death comes to all – but in America it has long been considered reasonable to offer the best chance of delay to the highest bidder.

One potential hope for the new American life is that, within it, such an idea will finally become inconceivable, and that the next generation of American leaders might find inspiration not in Winston Churchill's bellicose rhetoric but in the peacetime words spoken by Clement Attlee, his opposite number in the House of Commons, the leader of the Labour Party, who beat

Churchill in a post-war landslide: 'The war has been won by the efforts of all our people, who, with very few exceptions, put the nation first and their private and sectional interests a long way second. . . . Why should we suppose that we can attain our aims in peace – food, clothing, homes, education, leisure, social security and full employment for all – by putting private interests first?'

As Americans never tire of arguing, there may be many areas of our lives in which private interest plays the central role. But, as post-war Europe, exhausted by absolute death, collectively decided, health care shouldn't be one of them.

Something to Do

If you make things, if you are an 'artist' of whatever stripe, at some point you will be asked – or may ask yourself – 'why' you act, sculpt, paint, whatever. In the writing world, this question never seems to get old. In each generation, a few too many people will feel moved to pen an essay called, inevitably, 'Why I Write' or 'Why Write?' under which title you'll find a lot of convoluted, more or less self-regarding reasons and explanations. (I've contributed to this genre myself.) Only a few of them are any good* and none of them (including my own) see fit to mention the surest motivation I know, the one I feel deepest within myself, and which, when all is said, done, stripped away – as it is at the moment – seems to be at the truth of the matter for a lot of people, to wit: *it's something to do*. I used to stand

*My current favourite is 'What It Is I Think I'm Doing Anyhow' by Toni Cade Bambara, written back in 1980, which has the advantage of having a no-bullshit title and very little bullshit in the body of the piece.

at podiums or in front of my own students and have that answer on the tip of my tongue, but knew if I said it aloud it would be mistaken for a joke or fake humility or perhaps plain stupidity . . . Now I am gratified to find this most honest of phrases in everybody's mouths all of a sudden, and in answer to almost every question. Why did you bake that banana bread? It was something to do. Why did you make a fort in your living room? Well, it's something to do. Why dress the dog as a cat? It's something to do, isn't it? Fills the time.

Out of an expanse of time, you carve a little area – that nobody asked you to carve – and you do 'something'. But perhaps the difference between the kind of something that I'm used to, and this new culture of doing something, is the moral anxiety that surrounds it. The something that artists have always done is more usually cordoned off from the rest of society, and by mutual agreement this space is considered a sort of charming but basically useless playpen, in which adults get to behave like children – making up stories and drawing pictures and so on – though at least they provide some form of pleasure to serious people, doing actual jobs. The more utilitarian-minded defenders of art justify its existence by insisting upon its potential political efficacy, which is usually overstated. (Artists themselves are especially fond of overstating it.) But even if you believe in the potential political efficacy of art – as I do – few artists would dare count on its timeliness. It's a delusional painter who finishes a canvas at two o'clock and expects radical societal transformation by four. Even when artists write manifestos, they are (hopefully) aware that their exigent tone is, finally, borrowed, only echoing and mimicking the urgency of the guerrilla's demands, or the activist's protests, rather than truly enacting it. The people sometimes demand change. They almost never demand art. As a consequence, art stands in a dubious relation to necessity – and to time itself. It is something to do, yes, but *when* it is done, and whether it is done at all, is generally considered a question for artists alone. An attempt to connect the artist's labour with the work of truly labouring people is frequently made but always strikes me as tenuous, with the fundamental dividing line being this question of the clock. Labour is work done by the clock (and paid by it, too). Art takes time and divides it up as art sees fit. It is something to do. But the crisis has taken this familiar division between the time of art and the time of work and transformed it. Now there are essential workers – who do not need to seek out something to do; whose task is vital and unrelenting – and there are the rest of us, all with a certain amount of time on our hands. (Not to mention an economic time bomb, which, for many people, exploded within the first few weeks – within the first few days. One of the radical political possibilities of our new, revelatory expanse of 'free' time – as many have noted – is that it might create a collective demand to reassess and reconfigure, as a society, how we protect the rights of those whose work exists only in the present moment, without security or protection against unknown futures, the most obvious unknown future being 'sick leave'.) The rest of us have been suddenly confronted with the perennial problem of artists: time, and what to do in it.

What strikes me at once is how conflicted we feel about this new liberty and/or captivity. On the one hand, like pugs who have been lifted out of a body of water, our little limbs keep pumping on, as they did when we were hurrying off to our workplaces. Do we know how to stop? Those of us from puritan cultures feel 'work must be done', and so we make the cake, or start the gardening project, or begin negotiation with the other writer in the house for those kid-free hours each day in which to work on 'something'. We make banana bread, we sew dresses, we go for a run, we complete all the levels of Minecraft, we do *something*, then photograph that something, and not infrequently put it online. Reactions are mixed, even in our own hearts. Even as we do something, we simultaneously accuse ourselves: *you use this extremity as only another occasion for self-improvement, another pointless act of self-realization*. But isn't it the case that everybody finds their capabilities returning to them, even if it's only the capacity to mourn what we have lost? We had delegated so much.

It seems it would follow that writers – so familiar with empty time and with being alone – should manage this situation better than most. Instead, in the first week I found out how much of my old life was about hiding from life. Confronted with the problem of life served neat, without distraction or adornment or superstructure, I had almost no idea of what to do with it. Back in the playpen, I carved out meaning by creating artificial deprivations *within* time, the kind usually provided for people by the real limitations of their real jobs. Things like 'a firm place to be at 9.00 every morning' or 'a boss who tells you what to do'. In the absence of these fixed elements, I'd make up hard things to do, or things to abstain from. Artificial limits and so on. Running is what I know. Writing is what I know. Conceiving self-implemented schedules: teaching day, reading day, writing day, repeat. What a dry, sad, small idea of a life. And how exposed it looks, now that the people I love are in the same room to witness the way I do time. The way I've done it all my life.

For me, the cliché is true: only way out is through. Trying to preserve some 'space for yourself' in the crowded domestic sphere feels like obsessively cupping your hands around thin air. You carve it out, the time you need, after much anxiety and debate, and get into the separate space and look between your hands and there it is – nothing. An empty victory. At the end of April, in a powerful essay by another writer, Ottessa Mosh-fegh, I read this line about love: 'Without it, life is just "doing time".' I don't think she intended by this only romantic love, or parental love, or familial love, or really any kind of love in particular. At least, I read it in the Platonic sense: Love with a capital L, an ideal form and essential part of the universe – like 'Beauty' or the colour red – from which all particular examples on earth take their nature. Without this element present, in some form, somewhere in our lives, there really *is* only time, and there will always be too much of it. Busyness will not disguise its lack. Even if you're working from home every moment God gives – even if you don't have a minute to spare – still all of that time, without love, will feel empty and endless.

I write because . . . well, the best I can say for it is it's a psychological quirk of mine developed in response to whatever personal failings I have. But it can't ever meaningfully fill the time. There is no great difference between novels and banana bread. They are both just something to do. They are no substitute for love. The difficulties and complications of love – as they exist on the other side of this wall, away from my laptop – is the task that is before me, although task is a poor word for it, for unlike writing, its terms cannot be sched-uled, pre-planned or determined by me. Love is not something to do, but something to be experienced, and something to go through – that must be why it frightens so many of us and why we so often approach it indirectly. Here is this novel, made with love. Here is this banana bread, made with love. If it wasn't for this habit of indirection, of course, there would be no culture in this world, and very little meaningful pleasure for any of us. Although the most powerful art, it sometimes seems to me, *is* an experience and a going-through; it is love comprehended by, expressed and enacted through the artwork itself, and for this reason has perhaps been more frequently created by people who feel themselves to be completely alone in this world – and therefore wholly focused on the task at hand – than by those surrounded by 'loved ones'. Such art is rare: we can't all sit cross-legged like Buddhists day and night meditating on ultimate matters.* Or I can't. But I also don't want to just do time any more, the way I used to.

And yet, in my case, I can't let it go: old habits die hard. I can't rid myself of the need to do 'something', to

---

* There needn't be anything fluffy or falsely positive about this concept of love through art: the most apparently nihilistic or anti-sentimental art has still committed itself to shaping time into something other than itself, *and* to the process of having that something witnessed or experienced by another person – the audience – and this, to paraphrase Kafka, is 'of a faith value that can never be exhausted'. In the remarkable cases of Yukio Mishima and Édouard Levé, even the act of suicide – that most complete and final rejection of the idea of doing 'something' available to us – was yet capable of being refashioned into a work of art.

make 'something', to feel that this new expanse of time hasn't been 'wasted'. Still, it's nice to have company. Watching this manic desire to make or grow or do 'something', that now seems to be consuming everybody, I do feel comforted to discover I'm not the only person on this earth who has no idea what life is for, nor what is to be done with all this time aside from filling it.

Suffering Like Mel Gibson

The misery is very precisely designed, and different for each person, and if you didn't know better you'd say the gods of comedy and tragedy had a hand in it. The single human, in the city apartment, thinks: *I have never known such loneliness*. The married human, in the country place with partner and children, dreams of isolation within isolation. All the artists with children – who treasured isolation as the most precious thing they owned – find out what it is to live without privacy and without time. The writer learns how not to write. The actor not to act. The painter how never to see her studio and so on. The artists without children are delighted by all the free time, for a time, until time itself begins to take on an accusatory look, a judgemental cast, because the fact is it is hard to fill all this time sufficiently, given the sufferings of others. And besides, now there is no clocking off *ever*, and no drowning of artistic anxiety in a party or conversation or frantic exercise. Married men are confronted with the infinite reality of their wives, who cannot now be exchanged, even mentally, for a strange girl walking down the street. Her face, her face, her face. Your face, your face, your face. The only relief is two faces facing forward, towards the screen. New lovers for the first time wonder about love. Is love enough? Perhaps a dog should be added to this endless *pas de deux*? Or some other living creature? Young people hunger for the touch of strangers – of anyone. Club kids go to bed at nine. Older people, surrounded by generations of family, dream of exactly the same empty couch that is, elsewhere, right now, at this very moment, the purest torture for some lucky, desperate, fortunate, lonely, selfish, enviable, self-indulgent, privileged, bereft student. Married divorce lawyers go to war over who will work when. The children whose parents' divorces these same lawyers once arranged now move through the silent streets being driven from one isolation to another and back again, a metaphor for the folly of human relations they are unlikely ever to forget. The night-shift worker with three children under the age of six stops marking the border between days and nights or between one week and the next. There is only work. The single mother with the single child finds the role of child and adult passing fluidly around their small, shared space, with more ease and fluctuation than either party had ever thought possible. The widower enters a second widowhood. The pensioner an early twilight. Everybody learns the irrelevance of these matters next to 'real suffering'.

*

Just before the global shit hit the fan, we were in a long, involved, cultural conversation about 'privilege'. We were teaching ourselves how to be more aware of the relative nature of various forms of privilege, and their dependence on intersections of class, race, gender and so on. As clarifying as this conversation often was, it strikes me that it cannot now be applied, without modification, to the category of suffering. The temptation to overlay the first discourse upon the second is strong: privilege and suffering have a lot in common. They both manifest as bubbles, containing a person and distorting their vision. But it is possible to penetrate the bubble of privilege and even pop it – whereas the suffering bubble is impermeable. Language, logic, argument, rationale and relative perspective itself are no match for it. Suffering applies itself directly to its subject and will not be shamed out of itself or eradicated by righteous argument, no matter how objectively correct that argument may be.

Everyone has an anecdote about privilege they like to tell, a moment when they realized they, or somebody else, were seeing through a veil of assumption and/or relative ignorance. Mine is minor but I like it. Once upon a time when my kids were still small I was standing in line for a sandwich at Subway, with my son strapped to my body. In front of me, two women – who I took to be African-American and South-Asian respectively – were having a conversation. Nosey as I am about other people's lives, I was listening in. To my ear they were obviously working-class women, both with a robust sense of humour and plenty of lively opinions. They were great to listen to. And they happened to have landed on one of my favourite subjects, over which, back then, I frequently liked to ride my high horse: technology and children.

'I couldn't believe it,' the black lady said to the brown lady, 'I'm walking down 8th and here's this white lady with a kid in a buggy, couldn't have been more than nine months old, and here's this kid just sitting in there and he's *holding an iPad*.' The brown lady laughed, groaned and rolled her eyes: 'Oh my God. These people are really something.' 'Can you believe that shit?' asked the black lady, and it took everything I had to restrain myself and not join in this horrified assessment of the incompetent parenting of rich people, too lazy or busy to relate to their own babies, giving damaging mind-altering technology to infants. Infants! 'Nine hundred dollars!' cried the brown lady, with real disgust. 'Imagine giving something worth *nine hundred dollars* to a baby.' 'These people got rent money to burn,' confirmed the first lady, and together they laughed ruefully at the profligate fools of 8th Street.

The profligate fool behind them hung her head in relative shame. And then laughed at herself. In my privilege, I had mistaken one kind of ethical argument for another. An especially bracing experience for me, as only a few years earlier I would not have made such a mistake. Class is a bubble, formed by privilege, shaping and manipulating your conception of reality. But it can at least be brought to mind; acknowledged, comprehended, even atoned for through transformative action. By comparing your relative privilege with that of others you may be able to modify both your world and the worlds outside of your world – if the will is there to do it. Suffering is not like that. Suffering is not relative; it is absolute. Suffering has an absolute relation to the suffering individual – it cannot be easily mediated by a third term like 'privilege'. If it could, the CEO's daughter would never starve herself, nor the movie idol ever put a bullet in his own brain. Early on in the crisis, I read a news story concerning a young woman of only seventeen, who had killed herself three weeks into lockdown, because she 'couldn't go out and see her friends'. She was not a nurse, with inadequate PPE and a long commute, arriving at a ward of terrified people, bracing herself for a long day of death. But her suffering, like all suffering, was an absolute in her own mind, and applied itself to her body and mind as if uniquely shaped for her, and she could not overcome it and so she died.

Around the same time that I read that news story, I was sent a meme that made me laugh out loud: a photograph of Mel Gibson, in a director's chair, calmly talking to Jesus Christ himself. Jesus (also in a director's chair) was patiently listening, while soaked from head to toe in blood and wearing his crown of thorns.* The caption read: *Explaining to my friends with kids under six what it's been like isolating alone.* As a rule of social etiquette, when confronted with a pixelated screen of a dozen people, all of them enquiring, somewhat half-heartedly, as to 'how you are', it is appropriate to make the expected, decent and accurate claim that you are fine and privileged, lucky compared to so many others, inconvenienced, yes, melancholy often, but not suffering. Mel Gibson but not Christ. Even Christ, twenty feet in the air and bleeding all over himself, no doubt looked about him and wondered whether his agonies, when all was said and done, were relatively speaking in fact better than those of the thieves and beggars to his left and right whose sufferings long predated their present crucifixions and who had no hope (unlike Christ) of an improved post-cross situation . . . But when the bad day in your week finally arrives – and it comes to all – by which I mean, that particular moment when your sufferings, as puny as they may be in the wider scheme of things, direct themselves absolutely and only to you, as if precisely designed *to destroy you and only you*, at that point it

---

* I assume the picture is a candid shot from the making of *The Passion of the Christ.*

might be worth allowing yourself the admission of the reality of suffering, if not for yourself, exactly, then in preparation for that next painful bout of video-conferencing, so that you don't roll your eyes or laugh or puke while listening to what some other person seems to think is pain.

Screengrabs

(*After* Berger, before the virus)

A Man with Strong Hands

Midway between work, school, Three Lives bookstore and coffee there is a nail place. It is like all the other nail places, except in size: it's slightly larger than most. Given the nature of rent in lower Manhattan I assume this is a good sign, that the place does well. The clientele are mostly upscale mothers, well-mannered, generally quiet. They balance their iPhones against bottles of nail varnish, or read copies of *US Weekly* or *Vogue* that the nail technicians have placed in each client's lap, even sometimes turning the pages for them. The nail place has no decorative pretensions. It is white, clean, well spaced-out. The TV mounted on the wall is silent with subtitles, and the music that replaces it is unobtrusive.

Because of the amount of time they take, I have never had a pedicure. I don't think I've had more than five manicures in twenty years, primarily because you can't read a book at the same time. Any beauty treatment that doesn't accommodate reading – or takes much more than ten minutes – I find I can't accept, and so I don't do any of them except grey hair removal (which you can both read *and* write through) and eyebrow threading, which takes four minutes, and even then I sometimes try to hold a folded *New Yorker* above my head until the girl bats it away in irritation. My indulgence is massage. Like most people my age who spend their lives bent over a laptop, my spine hurts. But I dislike full body massage. (They take too long, they're expensive, you can't read – although I have experimented with balancing a Kindle in my hand under the hole in the table. It doesn't work.) I like chair massages. They fill all the criteria. No longer than half an hour, and you can read during – if you tear the paper tissue away from the sides of the face hole – and they're relatively cheap. Every other weekday I go to the back room of this nail place. And I make good use of my time there, if the purpose of time is to fill it always with activity, never to just *be* in it, nor ever to acknowledge its fundamental independence from your conceptions of it. I read some Berger. I mark some student essays. I mark up an essay I've written. I see how many tales by Tanizaki I can get through in how many twenty-minute bursts, over the week. I am a 'regular'. Nobody in the nail place knows my name but I am greeted with fond familiarity, like the 11 a.m. drunks at the White Horse Tavern down the road. I know the masseur's name. He is Ben. He calls me 'Hey, lady'. We don't talk much – not at all once the massage has begun. But sometimes a little just before. Almost always he says, ruefully, 'Hey, lady, always reading. Never relax. Always reading.' His head and face are optimistic in construction. He *looks* like optimism. Both his skull and his face are ideally round, he is always smiling, and he makes baldness look like an achievement, like something to be perfected. His skin is the colour of old paperback pages. I have assumed he is Chinese without asking, whereas he is more forward and asked early on where my hair 'comes from'. I said, 'Jamaica and England – via Africa,' and he said, 'Ho ho ho! Interesting mix!' At which point I should have enquired after the origins of his particular phenotypic expressions but I didn't and from that moment on it became too late to ask. Maybe he feels the same way about my name. His hands are incredibly strong. He takes each knobble of the spine and works around it, freeing something (what?) and the effect lasts for about forty-eight hours before whatever was free begins to knit itself back together in pain and I turn up on the doorstep of the nail place once more, papers or book in hand, and a few pens, and Post-it notes: 'Hey, lady, here she is. Never relax . . .'

We have two reliable subjects: the weather and public school 'days off'. The two subjects are interconnected. An excess of snow can close a public school and often does – too often for either of our likings. We also feel that too many people practise too many religions, the celebrations of which result in both of us having to scramble for childcare. We have nothing against God but we don't know what we're going to do about next Tuesday. We say 'my boy' and 'your boy' when we're groaning over what to do about next Tuesday, even though I'm sure I long ago told Ben I also have a daughter. For reasons of convenience we have settled into this symmetrical pattern. It is not the only false symmetry. The fact that school is closed for Ben's boy is a genuine emergency; for me it is an inconvenience only. I know Ben knows this, but out of what I interpret as his customary optimism and civility and desire to maintain symmetry, he allows me to complain with him, as if my husband or I cannot work from home, or lose a day's work, without disaster. As if me not writing for a day matters economically, personally, existentially, practically or in any way whatsoever.

How many beauty treatments do the fifteen white-aproned women and Ben have to perform each day of the week (10.00–9.00 Monday to Saturday; 10.00–7.30 Sunday) to make the rent on this three-roomed place? How high are the rents on 6th Avenue below 14th Street? High enough that the closed Barnes & Noble has stayed shuttered now for a decade, for as long as I've lived here. High enough that it's difficult to imagine how such an operation as this nail place could survive for even a week without the daily turnover. High enough that even when the nail place was two thirds full sometimes I would walk past (always being careful to cross the road to the opposite side beforehand) and see Ben standing anxiously by a hand-dryer, looking out on the street, his optimistic face transformed from the cartoon I thought I knew into a stern portrait of calculation and concern, at once mercantile and intensely humane, backlit like a del Piombo, and evidently weighed down by far more than, solely, his boy. Responsible, rather, for the fifteen white-trousered livelihoods behind him – and God knows how many more. There he stood, scanning for customers, hoping for walk-ins – or wondering where I was, maybe.

A Character in a Wheelchair
in the Vestibule

We're packing to leave and I've been sent out to get a certain amount of cash from the ATM, so that we have some to hand. I've brought a large Manila envelope. It's early days so I have no mask yet but I pull my sleeve over my hand to press the elevator button and feel outside of my body. In the lobby, there are already many suitcases; outside four car trunks are being packed. Most of our university colleagues are, like us, from somewhere else, and perhaps this somewhere else is where they are headed. Ever since I was a child my only thought or insight into apocalypse, disaster or war has been that I myself have no 'survival instinct', nor any strong desire to survive, especially if what lies on the other side of survival is just me. A book like *The Road* is as incomprehensible to me as a Norse myth cycle in the original language. Suicide would hold out its quiet hand to me on the first day – the first hour. And not the courageous suicide of self-slaughter, but simply the passive death that occurs if you stay under the bed as they march up the stairs, or lie down in the cornfield as the plane fitted with machine guns heads your way. I do, however, have a homing instinct, and so in my passive way have allowed a plan to be conceived: accept our friends' invitation to stay in their empty Kerhonkson cottage for a while, and then try to get home, to London, before flying becomes impossible. 'The last designated New Yorker' – that beautiful, stout-hearted conception of Fran Lebowitz's that I will read weeks later, while still in limbo, still living in Jay and Jackie's backyard – will not be me.

I turn the corner on to Broadway and find it empty – which is news, at this point, as I couldn't see it from our perch on the eleventh floor. The bank is dark beyond the vestibule, with only ATMs open for business. But it is loud in here because one of my characters is in here, Myron, from a story called 'Words and Music'. I haven't seen him since long before I wrote that story and I'm very glad to see he is alive and in such good voice, as it is fair to assume that a man in his position – homeless, legless – faces an existential battle most days. I don't greet Myron, because he is on the phone, because the time of fictional playfulness seems over, and because his name is not really Myron. Nor, as far as I know, was he ever a particular fan of disco – a trait I took the liberty of bestowing upon him. I have no idea what music he likes. Although I do remember, when it was my turn to push him down Broadway one time, he heard me singing some Stevie under my breath and joined in. And I know he is fond of conspiracy theories, which I have never considered anything less than an entirely rational mode of processing contemporary American reality. At present he is yelling and laughing into his cell phone, a familiar sermon I've heard him give before, in other contexts: the craziness of white folks.

Look at them scuttling like rats from a sinking ship . . . and what they running from? A COLD? These people are crazy. Just wash your damn hands! Ain't complicated. They out here acting like it's THE END OF THE WORLD. These people make me laugh. You see me running? I'm not scared of this shit! I'm gonna be scared of the flu? In what world? No, no, no, I'm staying right where I'm at. This is my city and I'm gonna leave for this shit? These people too hilarious. They watch the news and they believe every damn word like babies that can't even think for themselves. No, no, I ain't running from no cold. I survived worse. I survived WAY worse shit than this.

A Woman with a Little Dog

The funny thing about Barbara is she has a little dog whom she insists is a well-behaved dog but who, in reality, either barks or tries to bite pretty much everyone who comes near – except Barbara. New residents – grad students, adjuncts – sometimes believe Barbara and bend down to pet him, but we got with the programme long ago and speak to Barbara only, giving Beck a wide berth. Barbara lives alone, she's coming up on seventy, surely, and she smokes the way I used to: with great relish and evident satisfaction. Perhaps because of all the cigarettes, she is slender and often seems somewhat frail. In the past ten years her tall, elegant body has become a little more hunched over and sometimes she uses a walker, but not always. She has a tendency to list rightwards these days, like a willow, and her bone-straight hair, that swishes like a young woman's – and somehow always makes me think of Barbara as an ex-dancer – likewise now lists and seems permanently swept over one shoulder. Like so many downtown women she hasn't gotten older in the traditional feminine way, that is, by becoming in some manner less visible or quieter, less apparently confident, less abreast of what just opened at BAM or the Joyce, or what over-hyped musical just shit-the-bed on Broadway . . . And if you ask her in a concerned tone what she's 'doing for the holidays' – because you want to consider yourself a great neighbour and maybe deliver her a pie, or, more realistically, because you plan to sigh sympathetically when she says 'nothing' – you'll find she's just booked a solo walking tour up in the Catskills, or she's meeting with her radical women's group to discuss the writings of Anaïs Nin. She has a broad New York accent the precise borough and decade of which I can't identify, except to tell you few people in Manhattan seem to have this accent any more.

I used to think her little dog, like our little dog, was immortal – that it would be the last designated New Yorker – but then it did die and was seamlessly replaced by an identical dog with an equally bad attitude, and Barbara continued on her slow, smoking walks around the block and we continued to bump into her. Sometimes, if I'd published a piece in a magazine that day, or a book of mine had just come out, she'd start shouting at me from six feet away, repeating some small, unlikely detail of whatever it was that had struck her, but without any further commentary, complimentary or otherwise. So, I'd be dragging shopping bags back from Morton Williams and suddenly hear: 'Myron likes his disco! Yeah, I saw that one. Me and my girlfriends, we read that one. You having a good day? They say it's gonna rain later.'

There is an ideal, rent-controlled city dweller who appears to experience no self-pity, who knows exactly how long to talk to someone in the street, who creates community without overly sentimentalizing the

concept – or ever saying aloud the word 'community' –
and who always picks up after their dog, even if it's
physically painful to do so. Whose daily breakfast is a
cigarette and a croissant from the French place on the
corner, although to accommodate her new walker Barbara now eats and smokes on the bench outside the
hairdresser, properly intended for clients of the salon.
But no one minds because this is Barbara and Beck
we're talking about, regular in their habits and known
to all. There she sat on that last day – I was passing
with my little dog; a final chance for Maud to pee before
we put her in the rental car – and I could see Barbara
was preparing to bark one of her ambivalent declama-
tions at me, about the weather or a piece of prose, or
some new outrage committed by the leader of a country
which, in Barbara's mind, only theoretically includes
her own city. Already missing New York, I was keen
to hear it. Instead she sucked hard on her cigarette and
said, in a voice far quieter than I'd ever heard her use:
'Thing is, we're a community, and we got each other's
back. You'll be there for me, and I'll be there for you,
and we'll all be there for each other, the whole building. Nothing to be afraid of – we'll get through this,
all of us, together.'

'Yes, we will,' I whispered, hardly audible, even to
myself, and walked on, maintaining a six-foot distance,
whether to conform with the new regulations or to avoid
Beck biting me in some vulnerable spot I couldn't tell.

A Hovering Young Man

We look like we could be family – cousins. Transatlantic cousins. He is very American: super-enthusiastic, a little goofy, forever wishing a good day upon me. A self-described 'IT Guy', he works at the university library, and although he never gave me any IT advice (I never asked for any) he liked to let me know that the offer was wide open, any time, yep, any time at all. Once, during my first days in the city, I went for a walk in Chelsea and passed a brick-and-mortar shop that made personalized T-shirts. I retraced my steps, went inside, and fifteen minutes later emerged with a jersey top in two shades of brown, with BLACK NERD in large type across the chest. And this is the exact phrase that pops into my mind whenever Cy-the-IT-Guy accosts me (usually from behind) as I walk through the square, with his inimitable energy, slightly exophthalmic, puggish eyes, and irregularly coiled, unpredictable Afro, so like my own. The last time I saw him he was on a hoverboard. He appeared suddenly, speaking in his runaway manner, with as little preamble as he had manifested physically. If I didn't look down he appeared to be levitating by my side, a twenty-first-century daemon, or a surveillance officer, sent from some NYU central authority to shadow me as I walked.

I always tell my students: 'A style is a means of insisting on something.' A line of Sontag's. Every semester I repeat it, and every year the meaning of this sentence extends and deepens in my mind, blooming and multiplying like a virus, until it covers not just literary aesthetics and the films of Leni Riefenstahl but bedrooms, gardens, make-up, spectacles, camera angles, dances, gaits, gestures, sexual positions, haircuts, iPhone covers, bathroom taps, fonts, drink orders, dogs and people, and so much more – but people above all. Then semester ends and I forget all about it for a while. The world stops being so insistent. But this day of Cy on his hoverboard was right in the middle of semester and as he materialized beside me his vibe, his energy, his aura – whatever word is usually attached to the affect of a human being – appeared to me to be a means of insisting on something, a way of moving through the world, that was uniquely Cy's, Cy's absolutely, and which I could see with particular clarity that day precisely because I hardly knew him. Just as, when I first saw La Pedrera, in Barcelona, it struck me more as a belief system than a building, my ignorance of Gaudí being almost total. When we look at familiar things, at familiar people, style recedes, or becomes totally invisible. (Sontag makes the same point about 'realism'.) But in fact everything has a style – and the same amount of it, even if we value or interpret each iteration differently.

The style of Cy was youthful exuberance, it was a kind of giddy joy so irrepressible no doubt some doctor has marked it on a spectrum. It had something in common with those kids of my generation who took apart Atari joysticks to see how they worked, who remember no greater joy in a cinema than the moment Marty McFly rode a pink flying skateboard over a municipal pond, and yes, structurally, the style of Cy was probably not a million miles distant from Carlton doing that dumb dance from *The Fresh Prince* . . . But it was purer than all these because such secondary manifestations can only record, reflect and attempt to attract to themselves an energy that, as it turns out, is already in existence – in this case, the style of Cy that I'm trying to get across to you. I can see that it is a style that connects him with many other souls who are in possession of similar styles (and this family resemblance is hopefully what allows you to bring Cy to mind as I describe him) but still – in the form I experienced it that day in the park – Cy's particular form of insistence was unique. The style of Cy. What a precious thing.

It is easy to despise institutions, to feel irritated or constrained by them – I often do, despite a fondness for an ordered existence – but confronted with the style of Cy I felt glad he was at least tethered to an institution, like a red balloon caught in a tree, instead of floating out into the unforgiving city and finding himself deflated in the I T department of a bank or ad agency or some such. I used to see Cy (without him seeing me) from my carrel – bouncing around the library, presumably off to aid someone with an I T issue – and I'd often have the thought that an institution was, in many ways, a strange fit for us both. The best we could hope for was that the university might act as a superstructure, like a Gaudí building, accommodating and supporting our curious shapes and styles, and that this institutional cover would fool people into thinking we were something like utilities – and therefore something worth retaining – rather than peculiar manifestations of the spirit, seemingly put on earth to connect one thing to another, and to make said connections smooth, visible and/or usable for others . . .

But if we are cousins, we are twice or three times removed. Professors can be tenured. IT Guys cannot. The enviable style of the young is little protection against catastrophe. And the infinite promise of American youth – a promise elaborately articulated by movies and advertisements and university prospectuses – has been an empty lie for so long that I notice my students joking about it with a black humour more appropriate to old men, to the veterans of wars. Long before this crisis they were living with little hope of institutional or structural support, contending with perilous futures, untenable debt, fear. When, in the classroom, they insist on their personal styles, in a manner all too easy to find obnoxious – and causing the predictable generational friction – I have to remind myself to remember this: their style is all they have. They are insisting on their existence in a vacuum. A woman in her forties has lived long enough to see the dreams of childhood – hoverboards! – appear in the streets. She has lived long enough to see the social protections of her youth, which had not seemed to her dreams, but rather mundane realities – universal health care, free university education, decent public housing* – all now recast as revolutionary concepts, and thought of, in America (consistently by the right but not infrequently by the left) as badges of radical leftism. What modest dreamers we have become. But the young man in his twenties is still in peak dreaming season: a thrilling time, an insecure time, even at the best of times. It should be a season full of possibility. Economic, romantic, technological, political, existential possibility. Yes, among all the various relativities to be considered, age is one that can't be parsed. The style of Cy – the style of all young people – now radically interrupted.

---

* That were, in any case, imperfectly enacted in her own country – though more rigorously implemented elsewhere in Europe.

An Elder at the 98 Bus Stop

Is that Sadie? You don't remember me, do you? I'm ——'s mum. I don't think she was in your year, as it goes . . . Know your mum, tho'! Knew you when you was a baby. I seen your mum not long ago in the high street, looking well. She didn't say you was back. Yeah, we're doing all right. Still Stone-bridge, still in the Ends . . .

I had just got off a bus and was heading home, but when someone calls me by my name, by my *real* name, I listen very closely. I attend to the speaker as to an Auntie, as to an elder. And here was an obvious Auntie: mighty-bosomed in a V-neck T-shirt she had deliberately taken a pair of scissors to (in order to drastically deepen the décolletage) and wearing a pair of dark indigo jeans, studded with diamanté, skin-tight. 'Hugging every curve,' as they say. The whole back line of her body spoke of power and youth, although, by the local coordinates she was giving me – whose cousin knew which sibling's girlfriend at what time – I understood she must be an elder, even if she didn't remotely look like one. I took my backpack off and sat down on the paltry four inches of plastic that long ago replaced the sturdy bus-stop benches of my childhood. I got ready to receive whatever was coming. It was a bounty:

You know where I'm headed? Doctor's. You know why? It's this bloody menopause.

I sympathized, but as it turned out, I had completely the wrong end of the stick:

Nah, I'm going in there to DEMAND he brings it on! I'm fifty-eight! What am I still doing with periods? This can't go on no longer! You know when my poor mum got the menopause? Sixty-three years old. And there weren't no one in Clarendon to bring it on for her . . . She just had to suffer it. Not me, though, I'm done. I'm walking right in there and DEMANDING he brings it on, right now, because this is just silly business at this point. I got the fear I'm going be one of dem miracle mums on the news! Nah, I'm only teasing you . . . but for real: enough is enough . . . I want that meno-pause TODAY. Say hello to your mum for me, yeah? This is me – you not getting on? Oh, OK. I'm heading Crickle-wood way. Good to see you. All right, then. Wish me luck!

It's not often you meet a fertility goddess at the 98 bus stop so she stayed in my mind, as a symbol of a cer-tain uncontained and uncontainable fecundity, a natural abundance, which I suppose I sheepishly connect in my mind with Jamaica, with its residents, its diaspora, bougainvillea, hills, gullies, music, stories. A typical second-generation question to ask yourself: how did all that prior abundance fit into this new habitat? Into these boxy rooms on drab estates, these flats, these flower-free high streets, these narrow, rumbling buses. When you were a child, you looked up at your mother wrapped in gloves and scarf, shivering on the top deck, and tried to conceive of her earlier incarnation: barefoot in a pristine brown-and-yellow uniform, walking towards the one-room school house – but not too quickly, because of the heat – and stopping every now and then to smell huge, purple flowers. It sounded like implausible nonsense. Yet somehow it was true. Containment is terrible anyway, but how much more frustrating it must be if somewhere in the memory – even if it is only the epigenetic memory – wide open spaces remain, now utterly out of reach.

When lockdown arrived in England, I thought of this fertility goddess, and of the small flat on the Stonebridge Estate (routinely described, in English news stories, as 'the notorious Stonebridge Estate') that now contained her more tightly than usual, and of course of the larger Willesden maisonette that contained my mother. The strange storytelling of video-conferencing began between my mother and me, where two or three storylines run concurrently – you catch up on the latest every few days – while you simultaneously stare at your own face, a surreal new advance in human conversation that leads to the self-conscious adaptation of one's own emotional responses in direct response to how you feel they look aesthetically.

My mother's three stories were:

1. The PPE situation in her workplace, which, at that moment, was a ward for mentally ill mothers. (The situation was that there was none.)

2. Updates on the rest of her family, and
3. The progress of her half of the garden, which
   was going splendidly.

Pansies and clematis and magnolia in vibrant array,
abundant. *Flowersome*, as she puts it. And so it went for
a few weeks – no PPE, all family still fine, ever more
abundant, flowersome garden – until one day, when I
asked about my little brother, and my mother began one
of those long, confusing chains of local lineage, just as
the fertility goddess had six months earlier, about so-
and-so who knows oh-you-remember-whatshername,
who is the cousin of whosit –

– *and anyway, your brother knew her, she was in his
year, and her boyfriend killed her last night, in her flat in
Stonebridge, poor, poor thing – what? No, no, no, this girl
was YOUNG – she was in Luke's year, you're not listening
to me, you never listen properly. Anyway, this lockdown is
driving people crazy, maybe, I don't know . . . It's just so
sad. And then he set the flat on fire and it's been burning all
night.*

A Provocation in the Park

He was holding up a sign. People hold signs up in the park every day. Sometimes they say FREE HUGS. (Note to pretty Swedish backpackers: they're not free.) Sometimes they offer a service: tarot reading, personalized poems, a discussion about Palestine, as in COME ASK ME ABOUT PALESTINE. (Don't ask him about Palestine.) They can feature existential queries: IS WEALTH THE KEY TO HAPPINESS? OR IS THERE ANOTHER WAY? When it comes to the existential queries, there is a temptation to walk up and engage with the sign and the sign-holder, but the sensible park-crosser, who doesn't want to lose hours of their day, forces their curiosity back down and takes the long way around, past the burning questions, onwards to one of the sign-free, non-philosophical exits on the other side of Washington Square. Sometimes, the signs are for the purpose of professional identification: this person works with sand, or bubbles; these four people form a jazz quartet; this is the piano guy. Sometimes they are mass-produced and simply feature an arrow pointing this way or that, towards dim sum or cheap photocopies.

I don't often look at the signs in the park any more; they are too familiar to bother with, like the rats swarming out of the trashcans the minute the sun goes down. But I have to admit this guy had my attention. He was Asian, his sign was giant, and his message read:

I AM A SELF-HATING ASIAN. LET'S TALK!
Did I read that right? I went out of my way a good
ten yards to check it from another angle, as he walked
around the fountain. I read that right. Lacking a camera, I laboriously reported this sighting to a few friends
through the late-nineties T9 texting system, so that I
did not have to be the only witness to it. And I played
that pointless city game of tic-tac-diag-no-sis: Mental
illness? Irony? TV show? Provocation? Ideology? I go
round and round. I can be very dumb about things that
seem to others straightforward and obvious. I know, for
example, that I am meant to see very clearly that the
man who mowed people down in a van on the West Side
was an ideological terrorist while the man who mowed
people down at the Las Vegas country music festival
was 'crazy'. But instead I see a category called 'the impos-
ition of toxic narrative over phenomena' – the thickness
and complexity of which can vary while the fundamental character of the crime remains the same. I have
similar questions about murder as 'hate crime' and murder as murder. I find it hard to distinguish between
forms of hate that have the same consequence. The hatred of women versus the hatred of *this particular woman*.
The statement *The police are investigating this as a hate
crime* always prompts in me the query: when it comes to
murder, what other kind of crime is there? I realize
that's banal but I can't help it. I think what I resent is not
the recognition of a murderer's motivation – which

should never be obscured – but an elevation of importance in what strikes me as the wrong direction. To think of a *hate crime* as the most uniquely heinous of crimes seems to lend it, in my mind, an undeserved aura of power. I'd rather something else. *The police are investigating this crime as an acute abjection. The police are investigating this as a crime pitiful as it is appalling, pathetic as it is monstrous.* The hatred of a group *qua* group is, after all, the most debased and irrational of hatreds, the weakest, the *most* banal. It shouldn't radiate a special aura, lifting it into a separate epistemological category. For this is exactly what the killer believes. He believes he did not walk into the church and murder a circle of innocent people, *like a murderer*, no, he went in there to express his 'ideology' through the medium of violence, to commit his 'act', girded by what he flatters himself is a comprehensive philosophy.

Why do we take him at his word? We reprint his self-aggrandizing 'ideas' and only as an afterthought wonder whether his brutality is not, at base, the result of a hopeless inadequacy, both personal and social, even despite the fact that we keep on learning of the peculiar coalescence, particularly in young men, of the thought *I hate —— people* with thoughts like *I can't get anyone to sleep with me* and *I feel ugly.* But I understand the instinct. The crime is so monstrous it seems impossible the motivation wouldn't have an equal weight to the lives it took. Yet the philosophy is no such a thing. The special category has no weight. The manifesto is written in blood, and the 'ideas' that motivated the killer barely deserve the term. No, the killer took a base urge – hate – and robed it in clichés. *The police are investigating a hate robed in clichés, projected outwards.* Admittedly, it's a mouthful.

But I have wandered too far around the park to a strange exit. The Asian man was not projecting his hate outwards – as his sign made clear. His hatred was all for himself, and yet his sign was by definition low-level aggressive, because it forced all of us passing by to engage with his miserable thought process – as far as we could ascertain it – making it almost inevitable that we would try to interrogate it and diagnose it, although none of us had asked for our attention to be thus directed. It was in bad taste, let's say; it was a bad vibe, and almost everybody who walked past him rolled their eyes, myself included. But he stuck in my mind. Something about the way he walked, the way he moved through the world, suggested that this was no comedy sketch, no ironic comment, but rather a deeply felt provocation, meant to express a genuine thought process. A toxic narrative (to me) but one I had no trouble believing. As I understand it, it is usually considered a form of mental illness to hate oneself disproportionately, but unlike other forms of mental illness – *I believe the Devil speaks to me, I believe the government is controlled by aliens* – we don't doubt the man who tells us he hates himself.

Whatever else he is doing, he is telling an awful kind of truth.

The profound misapprehension of reality is what, more or less, constitutes the mental state we used to call 'madness', and when the world itself turns unrecognizable, appears to go 'mad', I find myself wondering what the effect is on those who never in the first place experienced a smooth relation between the phenomena of the world and their own minds. Who have always felt an explanatory gap. The schizophrenic. The disassociated. Does it feel like the world has finally, effectively, 'come to you'? That what you have been previously told were solely your own personal pathologies and conspiracies have now become general? What is it like to have always seen, in your mind's eye, apocalypse in the streets of New York, and then one day walk out into those same streets and find – just as it is in your personal hellscape – that they are now desolate, empty and silent?

About a month into lockdown, the man I had seen in the park sent an email to the entire faculty of the university, in which he expanded on his sign, explaining his condition as 'ethno-racial dysphoria', in a lengthy manifesto which, to give it credit, did have some of the aspects of a philosophy, and was full of ideas, albeit very strange ones. That made sense to me: when we are hating ourselves, far more thought is likely to be involved than in the casual hatreds we are prepared to project outwards, towards strangers. In the flurry of panicked administrative institutional emails that followed it was clear that there would be one set of consequences if this was determined to be merely an 'ironic' or hate-filled email, and another set of consequences if this was to be considered the product of a mental illness. I was glad it was not my task to decide between these options. Instead of the complex judgement such a decision requires, I was left with the useless thoughts of a novelist: what is it like to have a mind-on-fire at such a moment? Do you feel ever more distant from the world? Or has the world, in its new extremity, finally come to you?

Postscript: Contempt as a Virus

You start to think of contempt as a virus. Infecting individuals first, but spreading rapidly through families, communities, peoples, power structures, nations. Less flashy than hate. More deadly. When contempt kills you it doesn't have to be a vendetta or even entirely conscious. It can be a passing whim. It's far more common and therefore more lethal. 'The virus doesn't care about you.' And likewise with contempt: in the eyes of contempt you don't even truly rise to the level of a hated object – that would involve a full recognition of your existence. Before contempt, you are simply not considered as others are, you are something less than a whole person, not quite a complete citizen. Say . . . three fifths of the whole. You are statistical. You are worked around. You are a calculated loss. You have no recourse. You do not represent capital, and therefore you do not represent power. You are of no consequence. No well-dressed fancy lawyer will come running to the scene to defend you, carrying a slim attaché case, crying: 'That's my client!' You are easily jailed and easily forgotten. The stakes are low. And so: contempt.

In England, we were offered an infuriating but comparatively comic rendering of this virus, in the form of the Prime Minister's 'ideas man', Dominic, whose most fundamental idea is that the categorical imperative doesn't exist. Instead there is one rule for men like him, men with ideas, and another for the 'people'. This is an especially British strain of the virus. Class contempt. Technocratic contempt. Philosopher King contempt. When you catch the British strain you believe the people are there to be ruled. They are to be handled, played, withstood, tolerated – up to a point – ridiculed (behind closed doors), sentimentalized, bowdlerized, nudged, kept under surveillance, directed, used, and closely listened to, but only for the purposes of data collection, through which means you harvest the raw material required to manipulate them further. At the press conference, you could see Dominic was riddled with the virus – had been for months. Only his mouth went through the motions. His mouth said that he had driven thirty miles from Durham to Barnard Castle to test his eyesight. The rest of his face was overwhelmed with the usual symptoms, visible to all. Boredom, annoyance, impatience, incredulity. His eyes, refreshed by the driving test, spoke volumes: *Why are you bothering me with this nonsense?* Contempt. Back in February, 'herd immunity' had been a new concept for the people – or that broad cross section of the people who are neither epidemiologists nor regular readers of the *New Scientist*. But for an ideas man the phrase must already have felt profoundly familiar, being a seamless continuation of a long-held personal credo. Immunity. From the herd.

*

The officer had a sadistic version of the same face. *Why are you bothering me with this bullshit?* The bullshit in this case being a man explaining he couldn't breathe under the pressure of the officer's knee on his neck. A man called George. He was alerting the officer to the fact that he was about to die. You'd have to hate a man a lot to kneel on his neck till he dies in plain view of a crowd and a camera, knowing the consequences this would likely have upon your own life. (Or you'd have to be pretty certain of immunity from the herd – not an unsafe bet for a white police officer, historically, in America.) But this was something darker – deadlier. It was the virus, in its most lethal manifestation.

The immediate infection comes the moment the store in question calls the cops and the voice down the line asks after the race of this master criminal who has just tried to use a phoney twenty-dollar bill with the ink still wet upon it. To have any real chance of catching the virus from the answer 'white', you'd have to add a qualifier like 'homeless' or 'on meth'. The lack of capital would have to be strikingly evident – visible. But the answer 'black' immediately carries a heavy load, and a number of potentially violent actions – that would have been unlikely otherwise – suddenly become psychologically possible. You don't just lecture or book this type of body or take it down to the station. It would have no respect for you if you did that – after all, it is more than used to rough treatment. Nor can it really be taken seriously when it complains of pain, as this particular type of American body is well known to be able to withstand all kinds of improbable discomforts. It lives in cramped spaces and drinks water with lead in it, and gets diabetes as a matter of course, and has all kinds of health issues that seem to be some mysterious part of its culture. It sits in jail cells without windows for years at a time. And even if it did complain – without money, without that well-dressed lawyer running to its aid – what recourse would it have?

Patient zero of this particular virus stood on a slave-ship four hundred years ago, looked down at the sweating, bleeding, moaning mass below deck, and reverse-engineered an emotion – contempt – from a situation he, the patient himself, had created. He looked at the human beings he had chained up and noted that they seemed to be the type of people who wore chains. So unlike other people. Frighteningly unlike! Later, in his cotton-fields, he had them whipped and then made them go back to work, and thought: *They can't possibly feel as we do. You can whip them and they go back to work*. And having thus placed them in a category similar to the one in which we place animals, he experienced the same fear and contempt we have for animals. Animals being both subject to man and a threat to him simultaneously.

They have no capital, not even their labour.
Anything can be done to them.
They have no recourse.

Three strands in the DNA of the virus. In theory, these principles of slavery were eradicated from the laws of the land – not to mention the hearts and minds of the people – long ago. In theory. In practice, they pass like a virus through churches and schools, adverts and movies, books and political parties, courtrooms, the prison-industrial complex and, of course, police departments. Like a virus, they work invisibly within your body until you grow sick with them. I truly believe that many people are unaware they carry the virus at all until the very moment you find yourself phoning the cops to explain the race of the man you thought looked suspicious walking through his own neighbourhood, or who spoke back to you in Central Park, or whatever the fuck it is. One of the quirks of the virus – as James Baldwin pointed out – is that it makes the sufferer think the symptom is the cause. Why else would the carriers of this virus work so hard – even now, even in the bluest states in America – to ensure their children do not go to school with the children of these people whose lives supposedly matter? Why would they still – even now, even in the bluest states in America – only consider a neighbourhood worthy of their presence when its percentage of black residents falls low enough that they can feel confident of the impossibility of infection? This mentality looks over the fence and sees a plague people: plagued by poverty, first and foremost. *If this child, formed by poverty, sits in a class with _my_ child, who was formed by privilege, my child will suffer – my child will catch their virus.* This not-so-secret terror is lodged as firmly in blue hearts as in red; it plays a central role in the spread of the contagion. (To fear the contagion of poverty is reasonable. To keep voting for policies that ensure the permanent existence of an underclass is what is meant by 'structural racism'.) And it's a naive American who at this point thinks that integration – if it were ever to actually occur – would not create some initial losses on either side. A long-preserved privilege dies hard. A long-preserved isolation – even if it has been forced – is painful to emerge from. But I am talking in hypotheticals: the truth is that not enough carriers of this virus have ever been willing to risk the potential loss of any aspect of their social capital to find out what kind of America might lie on the other side of segregation. They are very happy to 'blackout' their social media for a day, to read all-black books, and 'educate' themselves about black issues – as long as this education does not occur in the form of actual black children attending their actual schools.

If the virus and the inequalities it creates were ever to leave us, America's extremities would fade. They wouldn't disappear – no country on earth can claim that – but some things would no longer be considered normal. There would no longer be those who are taught Latin and those who are barely taught to read. There would no longer be too many people who count their wealth in the multi-millions and too many who live hand to mouth. A space launch would not be hard followed by a riot. White college kids would not smoke weed in their dorms while their black peers catch mandatory sentences for selling it to them. America would no longer be that thrilling place of unbelievable oppositions and spectacular violence that makes more equitable countries appear so tame and uneventful in comparison. But the question has become: has America metabolized contempt? Has it lived with the virus so long that it no longer fears it? Is there a strong enough desire for a different America within America? Real change would involve a broad recognition that the fatalist, essentialist race discourse we often employ as a superficial cure for the symptoms of this virus manages, in practice, to smoothly obscure the fact that the DNA of this virus is *economic at base*, and therefore is most effectively attacked when many different members of the plague class – that is, all economically exploited people, whatever their race – act in solidarity with each other. It would involve the (painful) recognition that this virus infects not only individuals but entire power structures, as any black citizen who has been pinned to the ground by a black police officer can attest. If our elected representatives have contempt for us, if the forces of so-called law and order likewise hold us in contempt, it's because they think we have no recourse, and no power, except for the one force they have long assumed too splintered, too divided and too forgotten to be of any use: the power of the people. The time has long past when only one community's work would be required to cure what ails us.

I used to think that there would one day be a vaccine: that if enough black people named the virus, explained it, demonstrated how it operates, videoed its effects, protested it peacefully, revealed how widespread it really is, how the symptoms arise, how so many Americans keep giving it to each other, irresponsibly and shamefully, generation after generation, causing intolerable and unending damage both to individual bodies and to the body politic – I thought if that knowledge became as widespread as could possibly be managed or imagined we might finally reach some kind of herd immunity. I don't think that any more.

Intimations

Debts and Lessons

1. MY MOTHER
   Energy, vitality, charisma. The source: an undimmed childishness. Which I share.

2. MY FATHER
   A readiness to admit failure and weakness. An acceptance of guilt.

3. BEN
   Good humour. The family energy combined with a performer's desire to waste nothing, to turn all gifts outwards.

4. LUKE
   A home-made spirituality. Love of nature and faith in all natural things – including death. An internal clock that pays no mind to the time of the world.

5. MR RAINBOW

In his classroom, what was on your desk, in front of you, was yours to perfect. To do as well as you were able. Handwriting – even back then, a dead art – was to be taken as seriously as spelling, as maths, as memorizing the events of 1066. Joy and rigour were the same thing: if the whole choir was to get the benefit of 'Bali Hai' it would be by way of a martial attention to each part of the whole. There was nowhere to hide in that choir. And no pride to be taken in the fact that we, 'the singers', were removed from the school as a whole every Tuesday afternoon and presented with this task. There was nothing special about us to be found in that fact, not even when, months later, we sang 'Bali Hai' perfectly, just as he had trained us to do. Yes, we sang it well; the song was beautiful. We owed it to the song.

6. DARREN

That prejudice is most dangerous not when it resides in individual hearts and minds but when it is preserved in systems. For example: an educational system that proves unable to see a boy as a child, seeing him only as a potential threat. That any child who enters such a prejudiced system will be in grave danger. Be he ever so beautiful and talented, inspired and inspirational, loving and loved – he can still be broken.

7. KIBIBI

How to dance. How to make yourself up from scraps – from whatever is available. How to be continually surprised by small things, like the spring of a jack-in-the-box, your most treasured toy. Here he comes! Here he comes! And therefore: how never to be cynical.

8. KELLAS

To consider yourself lucky, even in situations which almost anybody else would consider extremely difficult and unfair. To think, reflexively, of whoever suffers. To forgive anyone who has wounded you, no matter how badly, especially if there is any sign whatsoever that a person has, in wounding you, also wounded themselves. To make no hierarchical distinction between people. To tell any story just as it happened, only exaggerating for humour, but never lying, and never trying to give yourself the flattering role.

9. CHRISTINE

That the diaspora included me. Sistahood.

10. MUHAMMAD ALI

'No Vietcong ever called me nigger.' Therefore: solidarity.

11. PABLO

A thirteen-year-old, avant-garde, painter appeared in school, very unlike the other boys. Out. Unafraid. From Argentina. The most recent immigrant in a school of many immigrants. He needed a model for a nude, which, in the execution, turned out to be abstract: circles and triangles. You couldn't tell it was me but we recognized each other. The picture was marginal, he was marginal, I was marginal. How to delight in a margin.

12. LORRAINE HANSBERRY

'When you starts measuring somebody, measure him *right*, child, measure him right.' Therefore: compassion.

13. JENNY, DRAMA TEACHER

A task is in front of you. It is not as glorious as you had imagined or hoped. (In this case, it is not the West End, it is not Broadway, it is a small black box stapled to an ugly comprehensive school.) But it is the task in front of you. Delight in it. The more absurd and tiny it is, the more care and dedication it deserves. Large, sensible projects require far less belief. People who dedicate themselves to unimportant things will sometimes be blind to the formal borders that are placed around the important world. They might see teenagers as people.

They will make themselves absurd to the important world. Mistakes will be made. Appropriate measures will be pursued. The border between the important and the unimportant will be painfully re-established. But the magic to be found in the black box will never be forgotten by any who entered it.

14. ZORA NEALE HURSTON
Just: *brass balls*. Although that's somebody else's language. The importance of finding your own language. *Brass titties?*

15. TRACY CHAPMAN
'All that you have is your soul.' Therefore: liberty.

16. HANNAH
Everyday goodness, care, attention, in the form of friendship, daughtership, mothership, siblingship. When did Hannah ever make anyone feel bad?

17. DAISY
Practical morality. A calendar filled with every birthday, every anniversary. Nothing put off till tomorrow. No love abstracted, instead everything made concrete and demonstrated. Memory and memorialization as an act of love, completed on behalf of all the other people less organized, less able to remember, and therefore grateful for the prompt.

The value of being that person who remembers the childhoods of others better than they themselves recall them, and takes it upon themselves to preserve said childhoods for safekeeping. Sending an old friend's childhood back to them at the very moment they are most in need of it.

18. ZULFI

To have one layer of skin less than the others, and therefore to feel it all: the good and the bad, the beautiful and the abject. Not only to make art but in some sense to live it.

19. VIRGINIA WOOLF

To replace that missing layer of skin with language. For as long as that works.

20. MAGS

Delirium, delight, youth, sunshine, love letters, love songs! '*Love me*,' sang the Cardigans, '*Fool me*,' and we did both – it was all we had to do. It is possible to grow disdainful of love songs of this type. But never to entirely forget what it was to hear truth in pop lyrics.

21. NICK

How to love. How to give. How to grow up. Laughter as a peace offering. Courage. (All intimations still in progress.)

22. DEVORAH

To make use of your missing layer at all times in all things. To read every line of a book with the same sense of involvement and culpability as if you had written it yourself. And, conversely, to write your own sentences as if you had no more ownership over the lines than a stranger. To be never finished thinking, because everything is as infinite as God. To know there is a metaphysics of everything.

23. DARRYL

History as the antidote to dogma. Identity as area of interest, as the form in which you've chosen to expend your love – and your commitment.

24. DAVE

As improbable as it often seems, it *is* possible to act. To lead. To use your imagination to build practical structures that will in some form improve the lives of the people who enter them. Paranoia about action – and the motivations for action – is the sickly indulgence of intellectuals and philosophers. The truth is that some people have a gift for action. In some people this gift is outsized, disproportionate, extraordinary to witness.

25. CAROL

When in the presence of a child, get on the floor. Or else bend down until your own and the child's eyes meet. Mothering is an art. Housekeeping is an art. Gardening is an art. Baking is an art. Those of us who have no natural gifts in these areas – or perhaps no interest – too easily dismiss them. Making small talk is an art, and never to be despised just because you yourself dread making it. Knowing all your neighbours' names is an art. Sending cards at holidays, to everybody you know – this, too, is an art. But above all these: playing. The tales of adult women who still know how to play with children – these should be honoured. Collected in a history book, like Vasari's *Lives of the Artists*. Instead, their grandchildren remember.

26. CONTINGENCY

That I was born when I was born, where I was born – a case of relative historical luck. That I grew up in a moment of social, religious and national transition. That my school still sang the Anglican hymns, at least for a little while, so that the ancient diction of my country came to me while very young, and fruitfully mixed with the sounds of my heritage. That the tail end of one thing and the beginning of another were both visible and equally interesting to me. Milton and Monie Love.

Hill and gully rider, hill and gully! Keats and Monty Python. *And did those feet in ancient time?* Kafka and Prince. *Yellow bird, up high in banana tree. Twelfth Night* and *Desmond's*. Malcom X and Aneurin Bevan. Oscar Wilde and James Baldwin. 'Pump up the Jam'. Peter Cook and Tupac. Queen Latifah and Vita Sackville-West. That there were so many voices in the streets. That such complex convergences were my earliest knowledge of the world. That no one interfered with me, sexually, as a child. That my father was dull and steady and did not drink, due to a weak kidney. That my own love of alcohol and all forms of mood transformers and enhancers for some reason never became excessive. That my mother had no hatred for her own skin, hair, nose, backside, nor any part of her. That my family was essentially matriarchal. That I was considered 'ugly' young and 'beautiful' later. That by the time the external opinion changed it was too late to create any real change in me. That the kinds of women I admired in childhood were all from what Toni Cade Bambara called the championship tradition: Neneh, George Eliot, Madonna, Katharine Hepburn, Grace Jones, Salt, Pepa, Lil' Kim, Joan Armatrading, Angela Davis, Elizabeth I. That my fear is stronger than my desire – including my desire to self-harm. That my grandfathers – one a violent alcoholic, the other a destroyer of women – were both unknown to me. That my brothers were a delight to me, from the first. That I was an oldest child, with all the shameful obliviousness that implies. That I met a human whose love has allowed me not to apply for love too often through my work – even when we've hurt each other desperately. That my children know the truth about me but still tolerate me, so far. That my physical and moral cowardice have never really been tested, until now.